Samuel Kweku Addison, a native of Cape Coast, Ghana, was born on 30th July, 1969. His father, Augustus Addison, and mother, Cecilia Ashong, together with ten brothers and sisters lived most of their life in Cape Coast until Samuel married a Danish woman and moved to Denmark with the wife, Signe Thorborg Addison, together with their child, Emmanuella Efua Thorborg Addison. Samuel's passion has always been: "How can I bridge the gap between people and systems?" This has taken him to many places and has earned him a lot of experience and insight like what we are reading.

I would like to dedicate this book to my family my lovely wife, Signe Thorborg Addison, my daughter Emmanuella Efua Thorborg Addison and my brothers and sisters who helped me along the way.

Samuel Kweku Addison

Music and Story Telling as an Agent of Change

AUSTIN MACAULEY PUBLISHERS™

LONDON • CAMBRIDGE • NEW YORK • SHARJAH

A CIP catalogue record for this title is available from the British Library.

ISBN 9781398439641 (Paperback)
ISBN 9781398439658 (ePub e-book)

www.austinmacauley.com

First Published 2024
Austin Macauley Publishers Ltd®
1 Canada Square
Canary Wharf
London
E14 5AA

First of all, my ultimate thanks goes to the Almighty God for making this possible, not by my might and strength, and I could not do this if He had not given me the strength to do this.

I would also like to express my sincere gratitude to Jude Fynn Annan who inspired me and had the idea of putting my life history in publication. The same goes to Isaac Kwesi Annan the senior brother of Jude Fynn Annan who motivated, proofread, structured and corrected all the scripts. He further on added what needed to be added to make the picture complete. I am most grateful. Without these two gentlemen, the work would have not been completed. I call them my editors.

My completion of this book would not have been possible without these strong and supportive men and women, Allan Agerbo, Keld Hosbond, Mogens Thorborg, Mrs Mary Victoria Annan, Robert Ayansu, Bernet Tetteh, Thomas Jager, Bishop Richard Ampadu Duku and Rev Dr James Commey.

Finally, my sincere thanks goes to all those whose names are not mentioned but has contributed to my survival and book writing.

Thank you and God bless.

Finally, to my dear wife, Signe Thorborg Addison, and my daughter, Emmanuella Efua Thorborg Addison, I say a big 'thank you' to you for your support and love during the formation of ideas and the stability in my work.

Thanks to all mentioned and those not mentioned for helping me and making this project a success.

Love to you all.

Samuel Essel Addison
African Footprint Foundation

Bridging Gaps with Music and Storytelling

Since the beginning of time, children have always been brought up with songs and storytelling. While it seems illogical to sing and tell stories to a newborn child who can barely comprehend the basic element of language, this ancient practice has been jealously protected and faithfully passed on from generation to generation.

Ever wondered why we sing to a newborn child?

Have you wondered why we tell stories to a newborn child?

And have you ever wondered why we calm children down and make them happy with music and storytelling?

Talk about music and storytelling, and you will be talking about life. If you will agree that you cannot separate music, storytelling and life, then we start from the beginning to where it ends.

Child Birth

In Ghana, when a child is born, a spirit is born, and like any spirit, it may choose to stay or leave the new world that he or she has come into. For this reason, a newborn child is kept from the prying eyes of all and sundry for a week. It is believed that a week is enough for a spirit to stay or for a wandering spirit to leave. It is also believed that evil spirits and evil men may endanger the life of the newborn who is most vulnerable in these times.

The nameless has a name, and so, everything has a name even before creation. The child being born will pick up the day he or she comes out from the womb as his or her soul name. This name would be a name taken after the day he or she was born and that is his or her soul name. This naming I call it the official root naming ceremony. So the child stays with the parents and only the inner family members with that name. Should something happen and the child seems to be leaving the world, he or she can be called back by His name. Otherwise, how do you call the child to return?

On the eighth day, the child is out-doored to the community. The child is then introduced to his/her immediate environment both seen (the family, the skies, trees and mountains, etc.) and unseen (wind, ghosts and ancestral spirits) and libation is offered.

To the skies above – May you reach beyond it.

To the earth under our feet – May you never depart from. it!

To the gods and the spirits of our fathers – May you walk blameless before them!

In the olden days, the religion and beliefs were same everywhere but now we have Christianity, which offers a little bit different way of outdooring a child to the community or to the church.

Naming

Then comes the naming ceremony. The naming ceremony can take place exclusive of the outdooring ceremony depending on the plans of the family and is attended by a few members of the family and friends. It is usually simple and a short affair moderated by an elder of the family.

To whom shall this child be named after? The father of the child gives the name of the child. The father bestows on the child the name of an exemplary member of the family or community. It is believed that a name defines the child's character and fortunes and that the character and fortunes of this member of the community will manifest in the life of the child. So names are very important, special and have a reason of choice and for the purpose.

He shall be named after my father, Ahenakwa.

Then let it be known that from today, you shall be called Kwame Ahenakwa.

The 'kwame' that precedes his name is his day name. It is the day of the week on which he was born – Saturday. A girl born on the same day is named Ama. This name is given right on time the child arrives on Earth as explained earlier. He or she takes the identity and will stay with that until the end of his or her life.

In the naming ceremony process, there are certain rituals that go on for the child to start the life journey on Earth. The elder who is steering the naming ceremony dips his finger in water and drops it on the child's tongue. He will then say to the child and to the hearing of those witnessing:

"This is water. When you say water, let it be water."

He will go again by dipping his finger in alcohol and drops it on the child's tongue. Again to the hearing of all gathered, he will say to the child:

"This is alcohol. When you say alcohol, let it be alcohol."

The elders often take water and alcohol, which has the same colour when poured into a cup or glass, and it is often difficult to tell by only looking. The elders know that while water tastes good, alcohol tastes harsh on the babies' tongues. This contrast signifies the two sides of life, good and evil. It is to admonish the child to support good and condemn evil. It also suggests that the evil and the good can also look the same, so one should be careful in decision-making and get to know to make choices and many more interpretations. The father takes the baby and offers blessings to the child. In a Christian home, prayers are offered and in the normal traditional home, libation is poured to thank the Almighty God, gods and all. That brings the event to a closure.

After the christening, the child now belongs to the community. We say that when a woman is pregnant, that is when she has her child and the child belongs to her but as soon as she gives birth, the child then belongs to the community. Each member of the community plays a role in the development and growth of the child. In actual fact, the wisdom in this is seen in most of the stories heard and that are being told lately.

Wangaras – Born to Die

We have heard about when a child is born, a spirit is born, and like any spirit, it may choose to stay or leave the new world that he or she has come into. A Wangar is born because he or she has been able to disguise him or herself from death and now can live on Earth or stay alive.

Some women will give birth and the child will die. This pattern goes on each and every time the same woman goes to labour.

From the very first day a Wangar is born, he or she was classified amongst a group of children who are followed by spirits and death, but this time, the family managed to disguise him or her to help the child live life. Wangaras, in the culture of my people, are children who are born to die, but parents manage to change their identity upon arrival to prevent death from taking them away. These children are known to bring pain to their mothers because of their refusal to stay put. This is particularly a big problem in the part of our world where fertility and motherhood are ranked high amongst all the virtues of womanhood.

Once they are born, their time on Earth is numbered. They are believed to be spirit beings who bring joy as well as untold pain to their parents. As if this is not painful enough, some go to the extent of repeating this painful process over and over again that they are sometimes believed to be the same spirit hellbent on inflicting misery on families.

Belonging to a fraternity of spirits, they are bound by a sworn promise to return no matter how well they are received on the other side. They first show up and win the hearts of their hosts and then suddenly take on a strange sickness. After days of non-stop fever and convulsive episodes, they finally vacate their Earthly body and return to the spirit world to rejoice in their exploits.

To bring these blatant and deliberate acts of injustice to an end, these babies were given funny names or were adorned with facial cut marks, which some call tribal marks, to make them beautiful and ugly at the same time, so as to be mocked by the fraternity upon their return and also to help the families to identify them if they should go by death and return. It was believed that this will deter their recurrence and perhaps encourage them to stay.

It is also made to disguise the child from the spirit of death. Death will come and will see that the child is not same because the child will have different substance on himself or herself in addition to the cuts or marks on the face and on the body. These will spear the child from being taken back. Then we say a Wangar is born. They often and mostly take the name Wangar in addition to their weekday name as their soul and first name. This naming happens as soon as they come out of the womb.

Would-be couples at the time did not have the benefit of medical technology to determine the cause of death of their children. Today, the incompatibility of the genotype of

couples is cited as the medical explanation responsible for the
rise in sickle cell cases and infant mortality at the time.

Values Passed on

At infancy, I was diagnosed with sickle cell and was given a few days to live. With resilience, the days became weeks, the weeks became months and the months soon became years. I have lived from grace to grace, surviving many obstacles and emerging strong, largely because of my beliefs and the support system that I have been privileged to have.

The elders pass on values through storytelling, songs and proverbs. Stories are told to inculcate in the child very essential social and moral values. The storytelling is more like a home school and nursing of common sense in one's brain to sound and well-educated being. This brings about special places and convenient places to be created by the fireside. This is where the old men or women gather children to tell them stories.

Proverbs are mixed with the everyday language of the elderly to stimulate thinking and teach life lessons founded on wisdom and experience.

That which I still recollect well and has helped me a lot along the way of life is the story of the lizard and the frog. This is a story where the lizard ate chili and the frog had the sweat.

It was the lizard that ate hot chili but the sweat from eating the hot chili came on the frog. The evidence of eating hot chili was the sweat that came out. The lizard had eaten the chili but it was the frog who was sweating. How come?

Let's get some samples of the sayings and short stories.

An old man will say to a child

"Woforo dua pa a na yepia wo."

Literally: "It is when you climb a good tree that we push you."

We, the society and the elders in it, can only support a good cause, not a bad one. Hence, if you want our support, you should do good things with which all can publicly identify and support.

Or

"Obi nnim obrempon ahyease."

Literally: "Nobody knows the beginning of a great man."

The beginnings of greatness are unpredictable. Hence, we should not despise small beginnings or condemn people when they are starting and seem to be struggling.

These wise words serve as a guide for the child who seeks to make a path in a complicated world.

Twins

It is more like giving birth to twins. Basically, the twins will come and will not be on the same tempo, so families have to work on them individually and together at the same time. Most often, one of them tends to be fast running and moving too fast on anything. The fast ones cannot relax much and for long. The other twin tends to be too slow and to act and move has a slow kick. So to help both, you will tell the fast moving one to take it easy and wait for the brother. And then, you will tell the slow one to move faster and move on so he can go with the other one. Even though you want both of them to go fast and reach, yet you slowly push at the same time to enable all reach the destiny as one. From this, we learnt how to go together with fast and long legs together with slow and short legs.

Stories and proverbs were told to us but not told whether they were for us or about us. We got the message and the wisdom out of it as progresses, No matter the type and the story told, there is always something there to pick up and use for life.

Songs and storytelling are a permanent feature of every activity, from the day we were born naming ceremonies, puberty rites, work, marriage rites and burial rites, addressing issues of concern to the people and managing issues in general, depending on the listener and his or her needs.

The Crab

Once, the crab had a head. He was amongst all of God's (Onyarkopons) creatures, the most admired and praised as handsome and friendly. He was openhanded supporting and helping those in need. So he will give anything you ask from him without consulting and looking into it. He won the admiration of many, and on top of it, he was just handsome and friendly beyond imagination. Due to this, the other animals borrowed his head to woo their prospective mates or to show off at events. One day, a friend came to borrow his head and never returned it.

This is why the crab has no head today and is constantly in a rage, hoping to hurt anyone who comes close.

This is a story that teaches the repercussions of having too many friends and not having the guts to say 'no' to them. It also has other interpretation depending on the listener and also the narrator what he or she will like to address. Stories like this have multiple interpretation and effects. You are to do good but you need to take guard and be careful.

Growing up

When the child is of age, puberty rite is performed to mark her entry into adulthood. The Akans believe that society needs well-trained mothers to bring up good children. Akans are a group of people or tribe in Ghana amongst others like Ashantis, Gas, Ewes and others. Under the supervision of the queen mother and some female opinion leaders, young women who have had their first menstruation are secluded and taught the secrets of womanhood. During this period of confinement, the girls are given lessons on sex and birth control as well as how to maintain a good marriage and dignity in society.

After the period of seclusion, a durbar is held where the newly initiated women are adorned with beautiful African beads and cosmetics. Young men of marriageable age troupe there to feast their eyes on the young women and to select their prospective wives amidst drumming and dancing. Rituals are carried out to invoke protection, blessing and fertility during their period of motherhood. This rite ensures that young women grow up disciplined enough to control their sexuality and to prevent them from premature motherhood.

Women are taken in high esteem because some of our great leaders made mention of it in this way that if you educate a woman, you educate a nation, but if you educate a man, you educate an individual. Therefore, the women in our part of the world go through lots of training and education.

The young men are introduced into the world of work by accompanying the elders to hunting expeditions as well as learning the rudiments of farming and fishing. Others enroll as apprentice in the field of weaving, carving, carpentry and others.

In all the activities mentioned, music features in all aspects of work, helping to reduce fatigue and also for amusement. The men and women both use music to go through all the hard and voluminous duties before them to survive a home. In time, the man is given his own patch of land to farm and earns a place at the table of the elderly where he will benefit from their long years of experience in marriage, parenting, commerce and life.

Passing on

Society was structured around music, dance, poetry, proverbs and stories. These were the tools available for the transmission of values, norms and customs from one generation to another. Every single child was expected to embody them to ensure that today's values were safely passed on to the next generation. This communal service was based on preserving the genealogies, historical narratives and oral traditions of the people. Records of births, deaths and marriages throughout the generations of the village were also kept.

The unconscious training of the younger members born into the community is usually through spending years of listening to the elderly, especially those versed in the knowledge of the community's history and tenets. To prevent the loss of valuable detail, the elderly painstakingly weaved their history into songs and sang it out to be learnt. This was a useful way of preserving the people's history, especially centuries ago where technology wasn't as evolved like now, and a whole lineage and history of peoples could have been forgotten otherwise. Even more so for communities that weren't learnt in writing or reading.

Those who excelled in this important phenomenon were revered by the community and were an asset to kings who regularly called upon them to intervene during disputes and succession. However, this role has now diminished somewhat. The death of any elder was a big blow to all, as it meant that a whole archive of history, values and customs has been lost. It was therefore incumbent on them to ensure the transmission of this valuable asset to the next generation.

Talking About Life

Talk about life and you will eventually be telling stories in the end. Human beings are made out of spirits, body and soul altogether. That makes us a special creature on Earth. The definition of a man alone can start or send one's mind to a dreamland where stories begin with the spirits, soul and body. From where I am coming from the beginning of a man or human is connected to dreams, spirits, the living and ancestors. These were also part of the characters that we see in our dreams when growing up and the same in the stories that we get to be told and grew up with.

The reason why I said when we talk about life, we eventually talk about stories is this. Life is defined more on what we do on Earth. Our progress in life is more of a story because our actions create habits, and the habits create character and that gives way to our behaviour. Now our actions categorise and define us under the character group and this is made through the manifestation of our behaviour. The story of our life in this world is the sum of what we have done and about to do with our life. Most of the stories told and are being told are all documentation of one's life.

In actual fact, the stories we hear are the stories that belong to where we are coming from. If the story told happened around your region, you will feel it and know it at once and will be able to associate yourself to it.

Kweku Addison

This writeup is a story of the man behind African Footprint International a non-governmental organization which seeks to bridge gaps between physically challenged and abled people, the privileged and the less privileged ones in the society through the use of music, drumming, dancing, storytelling and other arts forms.

When a man moves on in life, he then edits the past and rewrites history and changes the past. This will tell you how Kweku Addison made it by editing the past of his life by using the power of music and storytelling given to him by his elders.

Intro:

(Let talk about TIME and the FOOTPRINT we leave behind as we move).

Birth and Background

I am Samuel Kweku Addison. I was born and am a proud native of Cape Coast, the capital of the central region of Ghana. I was born on Wednesday, 30th July, 1969. My father is Augustus Addison, and my mother's name is Cecilia Ashong. I am married to Signe Thorborg Addison, and together we have a child named Emmanuella Efua Thorborg Addison.

This is my Story

I have seven brothers and three sisters including myself. Unfortunately, one of the sisters had a motor accident, so she is of a blessed memory. I grew up with my parents, cousin and siblings in Cape Coast, Ghana. One thing my dad did was to ensure the family was always united. Even though we had stepmothers, my father took good care of me and also all my brothers and sisters, and we lived a good life.

My siblings and I had great times growing up together; we took care of one another and had the best time together. We are all at peace with one another even till now.

Self-Discovery

My journey of self-discovery has been quite mysterious and interesting. Though fraught with challenges and peculiar circumstances, it brought me the self-discovery I had always longed for. For many, discovering one's self begins very late in life, but I was quite fortunate to have known who I was in the early stages of my life.

The adolescent stage is usually the most crucial moment of an individual's development, but I will say it was challenging to me but the best times of my life spent. It is the stage where one gets to know about one's body and also discover one's strengths and weaknesses.

At least everybody gets to know something about himself or herself. And I did as well. I learnt and got more insight into myself.

In my life, I got to know that I have more weaknesses, and that gave rise to many challenges in my life that I had to deal with. So I sought to work on my weakness, and in doing so, I learnt how much strength I needed to overcome my weakness.

Therefore, knowing your weaknesses can be of a great advantage to you if you are accustomed to the concept of persistence where your shortcomings show you how much training you will need to win.

I faced many challenges as I journeyed on the path of life. It was indeed a turning point for me. That is when I realised I had to take many things into consideration to help me live life to the fullest. The life I have today is because I have learnt to appreciate what comes my way.

A Blessing in Disguise

I was loved by many and resented by many in my early school years. For the many who disliked me, I took their resentment as vitamins that make one to be resilient. I learnt that 'in combat, your opponent always looked out for your weaknesses as a bait.' Therefore, dealing with such people helps you identify what you are not paying attention to. In fact, you will discover that they rather help you to grow because they enable you to fortify your weak spot. When I realised this, I paid more attention to know and understand what they identified as my weakness. I made sure to work on my weakness, and it strengthened me. Knowing my weakness at such an early stage and working on it helped me a lot. It has made me who I am today.

Fear as a Guest

I was told many unpleasant things, perhaps to break me or to make me stronger.

When the mouth speaks, it brings fear and unrest, especially when it is sent on an errand of destruction. I was not rattled because I knew the weaknesses that can get me down, and I have so prepared for an antidote already for such destructive and unpleasant messages directed at me. There were times people said I was ugly, I was weak and sick and that I will die at the age of 16 years and many more unpleasant sayings. For a moment, I was engulfed in fear. This fear was an uninvited guest.

I took this up as a challenge to live with him the fear and not having anything to do with him. I did live with fear and learnt so much from him. So when messages of fear were fired at me, I will quickly neutralise it so it does not get hold of me. The secret is that I rendered it (fear) powerless with positive declarations. For example, if fear says to me that I am ugly and I will die, then I will say to myself that I am handsome and I will live life to the fullest as my response to get out of its grip.

I learnt a lot from this encounter while living with this strange guest fear.

This was when I realised that attitude was far more important than fact.

From this stage, I started using more attitude to spice life up than facts. Though I gave facts the upper seat in my life but attitude was more important. There was no way I could change my physical appearance but I realised there was another way to look beautiful in the eyes of people. Your works define your looks in life. Setting out to meet the needs of other people and supporting them can give you a beautiful look in life and much more.

The fact of life is that the beauty that we see is not on the outside; beauty is from the inside. I worked on what was on the inside to make myself beautiful that is inside out.

The extraordinary zone is reached by crossing fear through the unknown. Through fear, I was able to cross the unknown, which is also a game of fear that plays against people who wish to move on in life.

Growing up, I didn't really know what I will become but with attitude, you get to choose your destination in life. I am very certain that there are many out there who find themselves in a similar situation where I did find myself some years back. Some made it and others could not. But if you are now realising that you are on the same road as I were, then this is for you. Otherwise, take some clues and add your positive attitude to drive yourself to life and living. I came to the realisation that the environment that we find ourselves in influences who and what we become.

The environment literally shapes you. It is a cast or mould of your background to life. The environment trains and trims you and then gives you a background that ends up forcing its way into your life. We all may have our aspirations but the environment and our attitude determines if our aspirations will become a reality or not. Our lives are seeds and the environments we find ourselves are the places where the seeds germinate. A good seed that falls on a good place will definitely germinate while a seed that falls on a bad place won't germinate at all.

However, there are instances where good seeds fall on bad grounds but still germinate because of the attitude of the sower in ensuring that the necessary conditions exist for the seeds to germinate.

While the environment that you find yourself in can kill your aspirations, it can also be the opportunity that can bring a change. The environment I found myself in was a challenging one but it brought the best out of me and moulded me into who I am today. My future was not very clear but I aspired to do good and serve humankind, and that gave me a good attitude to use the hardened environment to produce what I have today. The decision is in your hands. That makes life to be under our choices.

Walls

While growing up, my parents took good care of me, so much that I was not allowed to go to the heights of my education because I was not considered as someone who could survive the conditions in the schools and be independent.

To prove that I was capable, I finished my high school education a year before the normal time of finishing. I also started teaching teachers to sit for high school certificate. I got invitations to polytechnics and other advanced courses but could not be granted the go-ahead because I was challenged.

It was understood and accepted but under my attitude being a more important concept.

Teaching

I opted to teach because I saw teaching as a medium to impact the lives of people positively. I also intended to use teaching as a platform to tell my story and to convince others that they can make it despite their shortcomings and challenges.

I also wanted to encourage others and make my experience known to them to prevent them from falling in the same pit I once found myself. I would say that besides teaching, I had lots of plans in mind. There are some that I have been able to achieve and others that I have not been able to achieve. But in all, I would say it is not over until it is over. Nothing is over till it's over, so I still push and strive for the best.

One of my philosophies is 'to always have an aim and focus'. I believe we all need to aim and focus. To have an aim, you have to be inspired, and if you are inspired, you must strive to have an aim to it. They are intertwined only when you apply or use attitude in a right way.

I was very lucky to have served at the feet of pastors. One of the pastors who played a major role in my life was Pastor Richard Ampadu Duku. He was a great mentor to me. I learnt a lot from him, and because of my service and dedication to him, I feel emotionally attached to him.

Supporter

I have had a good support from my family and some friends, and they all took very good care of me. If you do not look at it right, you will condemn it all and conclude it that some of them were preventing me from my success by stopping some of my activities. No, it was on the opposite. How will you judge this? A school boy who could not lace his own shoes had his parents to blame. The parents will lace his shoes for him when he needed it to support him reach his goals, but at a point, the parents were not around, as the boy was sent to a boarding school. It was in the boarding house that the child found out that he could not lace his own shoes. This brought a big anger between the child and the parents. I want us to look at the help we have had on the way.

I can go over the hurdles in life. I can lace my shoes and do what I wish for. I can also go to the extent of helping others even though I am categorised as one who needs help. This opens my eyes to see those who have helped me in growing up as heroes and mentors in life. Apart from the pastor, my parents, brothers and sisters, there is someone who needs to be mentioned. I had one of my brothers who will go down to the pits with me and rise up with me. There is no hell that I went alone. He stood by me and helped me in all situations and slept in all hospitals that I went to and supported my fights to win. We started nursery school through elementary and middle school together on the same desk in classroom and were both lefthanded we were more than twins.

This is where we conclude that everybody has his angel and equal amount of helpers to help according to our load of troubles and hurdles. Mine was found from the beginning and that has helped me much.

Health

I was born a sickler, as the way it is termed. I had sickle cell disease. Many people know sicklers do not live life past the teenage stage. Most sicklers probably die before the age of 20.

Everyone around thought I would die at a young age. They always pointed fingers at me, that my lifespan was very short. Fear became my tenant once again. I have lived with fear right from the beginning, so there was no reason to be afraid. The thought of dying lived with me each day, so death also was never a problem.

A tenant can never decide for the landlord and that is how I overcame the fear.

I had inner peace because I knew my attitude will overcome the fear. At a point in time of my life, I decided to take a turn. That was the time I started using the utterance response to things that I hear to refuse all the sayings of people concerning my life. I fought against the fear of death. That was what helped me survive, and I am still surviving.

Attitude is Everything

My health issue interfered with many things in my life in different ways, but I made sure it didn't knock me down. I always said to myself that I'm the captain of the ship. I am the one to determine how I would handle issues that concern my health.

I am very optimistic and it is something I do not regret being. I have found lots of elements that have helped me in life. The key amongst them is attitude.

Attitude is very vital. It counts. I was once admitted to the hospital and I was told to buy lots of drugs for me to prepare for surgery. My condition really required surgery, but deep within, I knew that if I went in for the surgery, I will end up in the grave. From that time, I developed the thought of: 'You are what you think.' So what did I think of that time – sick or not sick? You are what you think, so I encouraged myself to think of what I wanted to be and that was the beginning of another journey.

I psyched myself to take in natural stuff, eat well and live right. This was a personal decision and a talk to myself. So I resulted in going the natural way at the hospital. I eat good and more. At a point, the doctors came to the ward on their normal morning check-up routine and I was checked up by my doctors and tested again. This time, the doctors were astonished.

They said the report showed that I was sick but I did not look like somebody who was sick. I did not behave like an ill patient. I was somehow happy by the response from the doctors. Now it put me on board to be under study by the doctors, meaning the operation had to wait for a while.

This took few days and the doctors saw more improvement, so they needed to discharge me to go home. The fact of the case was I knew doctors to be competent but this time, they were doubting their own facts. I was very glad that the surgery was cancelled because the doctors declared me fit.

The lesson here is that doctors speak about the facts and they act according to the facts, so they found all the facts on me that I am sick and needed operation. Then they made me to buy drugs to that effect. I bought lots of drugs which are facts to clean my system and thereafter go for the operation. Now I can ask you: if I had thrown out all the drugs, which are facts to cure to me at the hospital on the ground and walked on them, I would have been walking on the facts then and rendering the facts useless? Otherwise, if I use them as they are planned for, then, I am making the facts useful. All these are possible by an act of attitude. So we can conclude it this way that attitudes are more important than the facts. Attitude matters more than facts. Facts are facts, but when facts turn out to be negative in the direction of life, we take up positive attitudes to counter those facts.

Marital Life

The beginning of my marital life was shaky. I first got married to a Ghanaian lady. Before getting married, I got lots of counselling and support from pastors and elders. I also consulted my doctors and all those I trusted to help me.

I can remember my doctor telling me to make sure to search for someone without a sickle cell. The reason is if I wanted children, who would be fit and free from sicknesses, then that is the best choice.

I married a young Ghanaian lady. In my marriage to the Ghanaian lady, we had delays with childbirth, which took away all hope until the last minute that a child came. That was also another page in the journey of life.

The marriage started experiencing storms and setbacks. I would not say she feared I wouldn't be able to have a child because no children were coming forth in the early stages of the marriage but not that there is one. It was a worrying issue for me because I didn't want to lose my wife.

Thankfully, God gave us a child. A son was born and named by me. It was a free way to success. I was very excited that finally, we have a child. Little did I know that it started the beginning of an end.

Breakup

My joy was short-lived; just two months after the birth of the child, the family members of my wife insisted the child wasn't mine. I took the case to the Women and Juvenile Unit of the Ghana Police to prove that I was indeed the father of the child. I lost to the family of my ex-wife even though there was no DNA test. I took it easy upon the advice of the judge from the police department. I stepped down of claiming the child but wished my ex-wife the best of everything. My ex-wife divorced me and we parted ways.

New Beginning

After the divorce came an equal advantage and solution. My eyes were opened, and I found the most amazing and miraculous lady. She helped me come over my previous situation. Nobody told me to marry this woman but life showed me where I belong. I got married to this Danish woman named Signe Thorborg, now Mrs Signe Thorborg Addison. We married and had our wedding and live together with our daughter, Efua Thorborg Addison.

Our marriage is successful, and we're still together. I would say the marriage to my Danish wife has been much of a blessing. I am very glad I moved on.

Breaking Spell of Limitations

I was told I couldn't travel anywhere because of the state of my health, not even from Cape Coast to Kumasi. The state I found myself in made it impossible for me to travel long distances. I didn't understand why this was so because all my brothers could travel anywhere they wanted to. I purposed in my heart to refute this yoke placed on me because of my health. I saved enough money to travel to Cote d'Ivoire.

I told others about it, and that made me look very crazy. I became a laughing stock because I dared to do the impossible. That changed my name to be called a dreamer.

I set a date for the trip to Cote d'Ivoire. When the time got due, I was indisposed.

However, this did not deter me. After I regained my strength, I put things in place for a new trip to the same place. My sole aim for going to Cote d'Ivoire was to find the whereabouts of my mum's relatives. The second time was okay; no obstacle came my way. I was able to make the trip to Cote d'Ivoire by road. I was in Cote d'Ivoire for a month and returned to Ghana after that. This continued for about three different occasions where I found myself fit for another expedition. I was at peace with myself because I put my naysayers to silence.

Realising all that had been said about me wasn't true but could be a fact, I decided to take a bigger move which is powered by an attitude. This time, the plan was travelling to Europe. By God's grace, it was possible for me. I was so enthused that I broke every boundary in my life.

Going to Europe for the first time made me realise I could do anything I set my mind to. I was willing to help my group travel to Europe to fulfill the dream that I have set before us and that we will bridge the gap between privileged and less privileged, the able and disabled people through music, dance, drumming, storytelling and others.

Glory to God, I've been able to achieve this. Looking back, I've realised my life has served as an encouragement to many. I'd say my life has been a track as I always dream it to be, that others can run on to break limitations placed around them. People can run the race of determination just as I did to excel in life.

My heart is flooded with joy anytime I see that people can and have found hope in life. And I got satisfied in my spirit if I extended a hand to them. Everything around me has been a great achievement. Nothing in my life came on a silver platter. Besides, I wasn't born with a silver spoon in my mouth. I had to manoeuvre my way through the crowded path of life. All I've achieved was through dent of hard work, hope and determination. Seeing my daughter, my wife and many good people around me makes me fulfilled.

Casting my mind back, I'd say God has been faithful. I can boldly say I'm a game changer because I've initiated positive change in the lives of many. I can somehow say my life is like a story people can read from. I'm the editor of that story. I edited my past experiences to reflect the clean sheet people see presently. I moved forward despite the odds I faced. I always tell people it's possible. I always say people are the captains of their lives. They have the power to navigate their lives to their determined destination.

People should lean on God. There will definitely be ups and downs but they should persevere. The tunnel may be dark, but there's light at the end of it.

Music and Storytelling as an Agent of Change

Ask Why?

Ever wondered why we sing to a newborn child?

Have you wondered why we tell stories to a newborn child?

And have you ever wondered why we calm children down and make them happy with music and storytelling?

Join me as we embark on this journey of discovery together.

Background

Since the beginning of time, children have always been brought up with songs and storytelling. While it seems illogical to sing and tell stories to a newborn child who can barely comprehend the basic element of language, this ancient practice has been jealously protected and faithfully passed on from generation to generation.

Why has the human race refrained from questioning such a seemingly mundane act? I believe mankind has, over the years, witnessed and experienced the power of songs and stories as a tool in eliciting powerful emotions. To this end, when the joy of welcoming a child into the world inspires a medium for the expression of such deep-seated emotions, we have often resorted to singing and storytelling. As we sing our emotions out, it is unconsciously accompanied with facial and bodily expressions that suddenly resonate with the child, who responds by mirroring the emotions of the singer or the storyteller. This spontaneous overflow of a child's emotions is a sight to behold.

Songs and stories are effective tools for communicating to children. To the child's immediate family, it is a means of sharing a sacred part of them with the newest member of the family. Apart from its sharing abilities, it also serves as a window through which the child beholds the joys of the world. This inspires children to hope for the best as they begin the journey of life. Such positive effects are the reasons for the longevity of this ancient practice.

Stories, Music and Dance

Let us begin by trying to define music and storytelling. The definition of music and storytelling will give us a picture of mankind and its growth. "Music and Storytelling connects the body, the mind and the soul as one. Human beings are composed of body, soul and spirit. We shall try to establish its relevance to our topic.

According to my friend Robert Ayensu, there are four points that are vital and have effects on humans when we engage in music, storytelling and dance:

1. **Cognitive domain:** Listening to music and stories build children's cognitive skills. These are the skills the brain uses to think, learn, read, remember, pay attention and solve problems.
2. **Affective domain:** Music and Storytelling also helps children focus on emotional growth, developing attitudes and feelings.
3. **Psycho-motor domain:** Dancing to music and acting help them build their motor skills and allow them to practice self-expression."

The soul is where we process and develop our intellectual abilities, the spirit is the real mystical you, which makes you (your original version) and the body is our physical mortal body which houses the soul and spirit. However, the soul and the body work together for the spirit to make important decisions.

Our spirit is divine and can be reached by straight shots of praises, which music forms a part of. The soul of a man collects data from the body and relays it to the spirit for feedback. The spirit is the final authority of our actions and reactions.

These three units need to be fed for better growth and development. We can infer from the definitions espoused by Robert Ayensu that the cognitive domain deals with the brain training. For example, if one pays attention, that will be an act of being disciplined. Remembering, thinking, reading and learning deals with the intellectual reference system in the brain, a role played by the soul. The affective domain deals with the body, which interprets our thoughts (soul and spirit) through action by using the body. This unifies our body, soul and spirit. The psycho motor domain deals with our body. It discharges what the soul and spirit have through our actions and behaviour.

Human beings are emotional beings and often work from outside in and inside out. The system sends in data, gets it processed and then sends it back for an action to be taken. It is because the manifestation of our actions are as a result of our emotions. Our emotions form the source of our survival, action, decision, choices and reactions. If our emotions are fed well, it will manifest in our daily lives.

Music, storytelling and other forms of art have a way of breaking through emotions. The fact is that we are all emotional beings and have the capacity to understand and feed on music whether it was meant for us or not. Therefore, music is sometimes defined as a universal language.

I always think of music and storytelling as the vitamins of life because of their ability to activate our emotions. They are effective at any time to better our lives or otherwise. Whether there is a problem or not, happiness or grief, their effect cuts across all of lives' situations. Our emotions are a reflection of our decisions, circumstances and relationships with our environment. How well we use music and stories can be a great tool in keeping our emotions in check.

Storytelling

An effective way of inculcating peace and unity as well as share one's experience is through storytelling. Many of such important lessons and values that are at the centre of society's growth have been passed on from one generation to another through stories. They are appropriate in transferring values in their original state without any biases. This method has been perfected over the years and has proven to be effective in fostering understanding because it is laced with everyday activates which the people are familiar with. Stories can be effectively used today to address many of society's unbearable problems.

Stories can be broadly categorised into good and bad stories. For the purpose of the topic under discussion, we will focus on good stories. Good stories are stories that make you feel as though the story of your life is being retold to you or the storyteller has had the opportunity of knowing things that are most private to you. Such stories resonate with our source and elicit the purest of emotions which we have no control over. This sparks magic in its listeners and adds value to their being. Good stories will always feel the same no matter the number of times or people they are told to.

Aspects of Music and Storytelling Music as Foundation Builder

It is undeniable that a great deal of what tomorrow holds depends on how we raise the children of today. In Ghana, it is proverbially said that 'a child belongs to the mother when it's in the womb but belongs to the community when the child is born'. This means the child's welfare is a collective responsibility of all and sundry. This attests to the importance society places on the upbringing of a child.

In pursuance of this better tomorrow, society makes a certain input into the child with an expectation of an output sometime in the future. This is because society understands that what we put in a child largely determines what comes out. But the question is: how do we know which output to expect?

I believe that to effectively answer this question, we must first foresee the output we hope for and then determine which input will yield that output. Builders understand too well that in order for a building to stand the test of time (output), it needs a robust foundation (input) that can withstand the turbulence that will confront it. This is the secret of many of the old buildings we see around today. Therefore, to be positively certain of the output we hope to achieve, it is important to emulate the builder's philosophy in the upbringing of our children.

Children are the future, and anything that has a future must undergo the building process. All our inputs in the early stages of a child's life serve as its foundation. It is the first and the most important stage in their development process because if the foundation is solid, it can hold whatever is set upon it. Our society's future is doomed if the foundation of our future leaders is not well anchored in the values we hope to see in the future. While it may come across as mere routine to the learnt or tradition to the unlearnt, it is worthy to note that we can make the world a better place if we take time to understand what we are using to build the future of our children. We have the power to take charge of our own destiny. Be reminded that our actions and inactions have consequences. We must, therefore, put a lot of thought into what we decide to impart into our children.

Music as Link to Our Source

Where I come from, music has always been one of our trusted means of communication. As emotional beings, music has been the only tool that defines and connects our soul, spirit and subconscious. These elements constitute the source of our emotions. With the ability to connect us to our source, it is then possible to affect change with music. I believe that the gift of music and stories are our best bet in getting the best out of humanity.

When a connection with the source is established, the product is always good despite all odds. It is with this reason that singing and storytelling have a way of eliciting response from children even when it comes across as illogical to them because what comes from the sources easily resonates with the source. This is an indication that while we may be two separate individuals with different backgrounds, there has always been something that links us together as one. A classic example is that while we may have different mobile phones, we are able to connect due to a common network.

All human beings are networked to a common source, and the most effective tool or medium to reach the source are songs and stories. This is why the human race has always invested music and stories in children. The outcome we hope to achieve will be defined by what we assign music and stories to do with our children. Note that while the tools (songs and stories) are important, the content, which is the message, encoded in the songs and stories is equally important. So as we sing and tell stories, let us be mindful of the message we send across. Telling stories and singing songs are magical ways of creating a space for the child's growth and future survival.

Music as Our Background

For every picture we have taken, whether in good times or bad times, there is an ever-present feature, which is our environment. If what surrounds us constitutes our environment, then it is imperative to pay attention to it because it will eventually become the background of our lives. Our environment today is full of love, fear, emotions, beauty, destruction, etc. This is what will constitute the background to the growth and development of our children.

Our background shapes our life and helps to measure the growth of an individual. It is magical because it is unique, peculiar and special to every individual. While a background can leave a positive experience such as love and hope on a particular individual, the same background may leave behind a negative experience such as anger and pain to another individual. If a child feeds on only the deficiencies of his or her environment, it grows on him or her and then matures in the future as an Acquired Emotional Deficiency Syndrome (AEDS).

Our environment is full of the unknown. This has made man to live in constant fear, unrest and apprehensiveness. These are the colours of our environment and one can only imagine the background that would produce in a picture.

I will like both children and adults, especially those who are fortunate to be living the best moments of their lives and the many whose lives have been fraught with pain and misfortunes, to hear this word of peace and hope. This might be the good news that will enable us stand firm and go through the fear and apprehensiveness that has become a common feature of this world.

The things we say and do are what determine our emotional state. When we say or do good things, we are indirectly creating an atmosphere of peace and order which eventually forms the solution to many of life's problems that confronts us. Knowing what words to use and when to use it is the fabric that holds relationships and the home together. The absence of this is chaos.

Understanding this gives us insight into the power of music and stories in creating and shaping our environment, which forms the background to our lives. Because by grasping the power of words, we can then assign music and stories to address very sensitive situations to yield a desired solution.

Music has a power that transcends boundaries, beliefs and cultures. It can cut through any chaos or confusion with mesmerising ease in order to restore peace and harmony. It is soft and soothing in calming the nerves of the apprehensive and piercing to the conscience of the restless. Music presents peace to the entrance of our emotions.

Music for Altering Life

Until I discovered the magic of using stories to alter lifetime realities, it never occurred to me that there could be a time before time. I have observed that it is possible to edit the timelines of life already spent and about to be spend. I have also seen that the end of a good story is often that which gives the possibility of the beginning of the same story. If this sounds like a story or a song to your ear, it is because it is so. Life is an unfolding story to be told and retold.

I grew up with time, and with time I was made to understand that 'time' cannot be reversed once it has been spent. This age-old belief has made it difficult for many to be flexible in life because it has been drummed into their heads that time lost can never be regained. Some go to the extent of punishing themselves because they feel time has passed them by. In Europe, when one arrives a minute after the train leaves, they will say, "Oh, I am late." Sometimes, this can set off a chain reaction of disappointments and anxiety. However, in Africa, a person in the same context will say, "Oh, the train left me." He/she will not feel bad but will wait for the next train to honour his/her appointment.

Is the difference in response to the result of different stories fed to us? Let us consider the following analogies with the hope of finding answers.

In Europe, time is planned in advance. Every second of every minute is scheduled ahead of time. However, in Africa, we live and spend time even before time begins. Time to an African is defined by one's readiness. It is when one is ready that time begins. An example is when my brother's child came to Denmark and was surprised to see a bus take off when it wasn't filled to capacity. We eventually had to convince him that the bus left because it was time to leave. The reasons for his inquisitions was simple; in Africa, where he comes from, the bus only leaves when the last person arrives. A bus that is scheduled to leave at 10:00 will leave at 9:00 if all the passengers are present. Or it will leave at 11:00 if they are already at that time. So until the last person is ready is when time starts. These philosophies are not taught but the child grows up knowing.

How do they learn and form such philosophies? Do you think music, dance and storytelling have a role to play in their orientation?

Before we were born, the story of our lives had already been running. From the race as a sperm and our eventual victory to join the journey of life, we have justified our place in the story of life as victors and winners.

Ask any African child the meaning of his name and you will discover the story before his/her birth. In Ghana, a child is born a spirit, and like any spirit, it is believed that it may choose to stay or leave. For this reason, I was kept away from the prying eyes of all and sundry for a week and entertained through songs and stories. It is believed that a week is enough for a spirit to decide to stay or for a wandering spirit to leave. On the eighth day, I was out-doored to the community. I was introduced to my immediate environment both seen (the families, the skies, trees, mountains, etc.) and unseen (wind, ghosts and ancestral spirits) and libation was offered.

My name was already known and prepared before my birth. It was as though they knew I will win the race in my mother's womb in order to enter the world to manifest the story foretold of my life. While a name can give meaning to one's existence, it can also be the source of misfortune. Once born, life changes hand. Like a relay race, the newborn takes the baton to continue the story foretold (before his/her arrival). The child runs the race of life to the best of his/her knowledge and understanding. Fully in charge, it is incumbent of the runner to take control of his/her life and decide how to run the race set before him/her.

Life is beautiful when you know how to edit time. I created the timeline I find myself today in because I could not walk in the unbearable storyline made for me. I took charge of my story and decided to run the race my own way. Knowing this changed my life and brought a new meaning to it.

I have learnt a lot from the stories I was exposed to. The most important one is understanding that attitude is more important than facts in the race of life. Attitude determines whether facts will matter or not. While many wonder how I took my destiny into my own hands, I have always maintained that everybody is a story being told, and like any story, there is a storyline in which the storyteller is free to edit to satisfy his/her desired end. This makes music and storytelling very special tools to focus and use in life's upbringing. We all have the same foundation, and it is possible for all to do what I have done in their own way.

Assigning Music and Storytelling The Blind

Once in a conversation between a blind man and his friend with full vision, the blind man noticed that there had been lights out. This lights out together with dark clouds had created such an unbearable darkness that the blind man's friend could not help but complain about how he had been rendered inactive. His utterance surprised the blind man who knew that even with his lack of sight, he had not been limited in any way. At this point, the blind man could do and reach more than his friend with vision.

Sometimes, our ears have the potential of giving us sight and making us see clearly when we feed them with good stories and songs. Have you wondered how the blind are able to describe things around them with amazing detail and accuracy even with their lack of sight? Telling stories and singing to them enable their soul to reach out to their sensors, which open their subconscious mind to see things that people with vision cannot see.

We can, therefore, conclude that music and storytelling reach people according to their individual needs and challenges as well as function differently from person to person. Such unique attributes of music and storytelling are what make them special.

Life At Home

From my little village, I grew up seeing married women struggle to find an appropriate means of settling their marital problems. Knowing that problems needed to be confronted in order to be solved, they also feared that this attempt to ensure peace, if not well handled, might be misconstrued as confrontational and might worsen an already-bad situation. This dilemma compels them to seek solace in songs and stories.

Songs are composed with a familiar melody and lyrics that discuss the problem at hand. They envisage that as they sing out the songs over and over again, the soothing nature of the melody will calm the nerves of the husband as well as draw his attention to its lyrics. When the target is reached, its manifestation is clear for all to see. The problem is settled quietly, and peace prevails in the home. Once again, music is assigned a duty, which is to promote peace in the home, and it delivers with perfection. We create, celebrate, disseminate, mourn and enjoy life with music, dance and storytelling. Life begins and ends with music and stories in all cultures of the world. Looking back to what music is doing and can do encourages me to highlight some of these stories to enable you to understand the power of music and storytelling.

Road of Life

I used to be very shy when I was growing up. It was so unbearable that conveying my emotions or expressing my opinions to my peers was a challenge. Whether it was a stage in life or had something to do with my age, I had to learn how to overcome it. I started to figure out new ways to get things done. I was fortunate to remember most of the stories and songs used to address situations when I was growing up. These experiences from home were a veritable source of help to me. It helped me to develop interest in listening and telling stories.

When I was of young age and there was a need to have a partner, proposing love was always a difficult affair. So I drew inspiration from what I was used to at the time. I composed a song with a familiar melody and lyrics that expressed my feelings of love. To be certain of its effects, I interlaced a story into the song. When the time came, I sang out the song to her. It was amazing to see the effects right before my eyes even before she could utter a word. The feedback in her bodily expressions of smiles and joy were so clear; I knew she had accepted my proposal.

The Landlord

Another unforgettable experience I had with music was when I lived in a rented apartment with my partner in Downtown Aquarium, a suburb of Cape Coast. This was my first attempt at finding independence after leaving home. Due to the disrespectful attitude of the landlord towards the tenants, many tenants lived quietly with resentments. One person who could not tolerate this charade was my next door neighbour who had just moved to the city from the village.

He began an exercise to give the landlord a dose of his own medicine. This was a risky endeavour because a confrontation with the landlord could result in an eviction. This was something many tenants had considered and had kept silence. Fed up with this attitude, this tenant bought a record of a popular musician at the time, known for composing songs about real life situations. The lyrics of one of the songs read:

"Houses are not like boxes
For if houses were like boxes
I would travel with my own…"

His intentions were clear and simple. As travellers, we all have houses from where we came from, we have become tenants because it is practically impossible to travel with our houses. He strategically played the song over and over again to ensure it drew the attention of the landlord to the message conveyed in the song.

In time, as the landlord paid attention, he got the message and knew it was directed at him. The landlord recognised the unfair treatment he meted out to the tenants and then apologised for his actions. After that incident, peace prevailed, and we lived happily together. Though it was just a song, it went straight to where it had been sent to and came back with a positive response. This is the power of music and stories.

My Experience with Music

Growing up with music at every stage of my life made me understand what music does in preparing the foundation of what is at stake. At least, I learnt that music can be beneficial to the troubled mind as well as the untroubled mind if you use it to reach that purpose. I have experienced this myself.

One day, I went to a certain village to find a piece of land to buy so I can build a house for my family in the future. When I arrived at the location, I realised this little community needed support. Majority of the children were either school dropouts or never attended school because their parents could not afford. This was evident in the level of poverty of the place. I felt I could not stay in the area if there was no place for creating awareness and education.

At the time, I had started the movement called African Footprint International, which sought to bridge the gap between the physically challenged and abled people, privileged and less privileged in the society through music, dance, storytelling and other educative activities. Eventually, the community became a place for me to prove that the tools of music, drumming, dancing and storytelling can bring about development.

Development with Storytelling

The hurdle was how to bring about development through the tools of music, drumming, dancing and storytelling. The least was to open the opportunity for the children between the age of zero to the age of seven to go to school while figuring out something for the grownups to sustain themselves and be able to take care of their children and families. There were elders and wise people in the place, so we couldn't just show up and tell them anything. We needed a well-thought-out plan.

We planned a music and dance event in the centre of the village where African Footprint International drummers and dancers performed a sketch about the problems of the community as well as its solution. This brought the whole community to the village square. After our performances, it was much easier for me to ask questions and tell stories around the performance. For a moment, the environment was akin to a school with both the young and elderly learning to bring a change in their community.

The project went well, resulting in the start of the Footprint Vocational Training Centre and also Footprint Child Development Centre for the village without any hindrances.

Listening to stories and music increased my sense of judgment and gave me more room to operate. It gave me patterns and enough information as references to situations and cases that I found myself into.

Let me bring back the lizard and the frog situation where the lizard ate chili and the frog was becoming the one to sweat. How can you explain this? I can tell you another story to end this project.

Donkey's Problem

The great Bentil was a king in Golden Greenhill Village. The king lived with a donkey, goats, sheep, cows, fowls, pigs and others. The king also had a wonderful cat that followed him wherever he went. The king had one daughter whom he loved so much. He sent his daughter to a school in a far, far away village to be trained as a doctor.

In the village, all the animals ate to their satisfaction until a time that the king travelled to visit his daughter at her school. Then all the animals started feeling starved. They were not given enough food to eat. Most of the animals started thinking of how to survive, and that made them to decide a way that they could store food to eat. From that time, the donkey, together with the goat and the other animals, started learning how to store food in their mouth while eating so that they could store food for later. This they will store in their mouth and will be eating until the next food will come.

The donkey was special in that he could store more food in his mouth, so he was never hungry. The donkey would start throwing his legs in the sky whenever he had eaten and was satisfied. The donkey would sleep with his back on the floor and throw up his legs in the skies and fool. The donkey continued this behaviour for some time, and that made the cat to be concerned. He had been watching the donkey and said to the goat one day that the donkey's foolishness might put all of them in trouble, so he went ahead to advice the donkey to stop throwing his legs and stop fooling. The donkey did not mind the cat but rather told the cat that he was jealous about him being happy.

The cat was worried, so he went to the goat and told him about the donkey's behaviour, that anytime that he finished eating, he threw his legs in the air and, at dangerous activities, could cause a problem for them all. He continued to say that he had already talked to the donkey about his behaviour but the donkey refused to listen. The cat asked the goat if he could help get the donkey to stop misbehaving. The goat got up and shouted at the cat, "I think you are worrying yourself too much. Donkey is old enough that if he gets problem, it is him that will answer for it, not you, cat! So he cannot tell him anything."

The fowl chicken, hen and the pig were also contacted by the cat, and they also got up and said to the cat that even if the donkey should get a problem, it would not be their problem but donkey's own. The cow and even the lamb said the same. None of them supported the cat's idea of advising the donkey to put a stop to his bad behaviour.

As the days went by, the donkey kept on doing what he called happiness by throwing his legs and hands everywhere possible with his back on the ground. One day, King Bentsil came back home from his trip with his daughter, as she was on mid-term, a short break from school. When the daughter came home, for the first time she saw the donkey in his happy mood, as the donkey called it. The daughter was surprised because that was her first time of seeing donkey act like that.

She decided to go closer to see what exactly the donkey was doing. When she went closer, unfortunately, the donkey threw his legs into the king's daughter's stomach. The girl fell down and collapsed there and then.

"Help, help! Somebody, help!" shouted the king's servants. "People should come. People should come." The king came out of his room and saw that his daughter had collapsed and was lying on the floor. The king was very sad because he loved his daughter very much and would do anything to save her. Quickly, he called the donkey to take the daughter to the doctor who was in the next two towns – far away. They had to hurry up before the girl died. As there were no cars or any means of transport, it was obvious that the donkey was the same one to carry her to the doctor in that village far away.

The donkey took the girl and started running to the doctor. The donkey had to run faster, and as he couldn't go faster than he was doing, he started receiving some whips to push him to run faster because the king wanted to make sure that the daughter survived. He was ready to sacrifice anything for his daughter's life. The donkey really suffered before reaching the hospital. Unfortunately, when they arrived at the hospital, the girl was dead. The donkey had to return the girl back to the village and tell the family what had happened. When he came back, all the other animals pitied him because he was bleeding so much from the whips that he received. All his shoes were torn off due to the running and the long-distance travelling. All his body had cuts with lots of blood coming down as a result from the whipping.

The king announced the death of his daughter and also announced the funeral date. Then came the day of the funeral for the king's daughter. The king indeed loved his daughter, so he said to his servants that they should prepare more food and meat for those who would come and mourn with him. The king ordered the servants to slaughter the fowls, goats, sheep, pigs and other animals for the funeral celebration because he would like to have more meat for those helping him mourn his daughter.

The king's servants lined up the animals – fowls, pigs, goats, sheep and the rest towards the slaughterhouse. They looked very sad because they knew what was going to happen to them. Then from nowhere came the cat. He saw the sad faces of his friends. He asked what was happening. They told the cat that they were going to the slaughterhouse.

He asked, "What did you do that you have to go to the slaughterhouse now?" They replied that they had done nothing. Then the cat further asked, "Then why are you going?" They replied that it was because of the king's daughter's death. The cat then asked them, "Were you the ones who killed her?"

They said, "No."

The cat then said to them, "But you told me that when the donkey gets any problem, he would have to solve it himself; it will not be you who will have to answer and solve his problems for him. But now look at you. The donkey is walking free and you are going to be killed for the party."

It was the lizard that ate hot chili but the sweat from eating the hot chili came on the frog. The evidence of eating hot chili was the sweat that came out. The lizard had eaten the chili but it was the frog who was sweating.

We often use stories to answer a story and solve a story's complications. So now, how come the lizard ate the chili and the frog became the one to sweat is explained. Try and figure out from the donkey's problem story above.

Conclusion

If we all share the efficacy of music and stories in curing the evils of our society, why have we not prioritised them in our daily activities? Many institutions today have long relegated or are in the process of relegating music to the background. When our emotions are deficient, a vacuum is created in the deepest part of our existence because our emotions are connected to the source. This is the reason for the emotional instability amongst the youth. When the tree corrupts, it bears no good fruits.

It is obvious that the solution is reintroducing music and stories back into our everyday lives for remedying the wrongs of society, for teaching values and for promoting peace and harmony.

Music and storytelling has been used to welcome children into the society. We need to keep up as the basic measure of our life. This will form the solid background that will ensure that our future will be in good hands.

When the stories are told, we can tell and preach every truth that is difficult to say and pronounce. We can address authority and send in request without stepping on any toe, and we can reach our goal in peace.

I still believe the use of music and storytelling is the gateway to offer emotional support and to affect corrections in society and the world at large. If we should touch the ethics and morals of a society, it could be reached through a story. Let us task music and stories to do what other tools have failed to do. Let's give it a message of peace and hope to consul, encourage and to foster togetherness. Let's use it as a tool for leadership development and as an agent of change for our future leaders.